W9-BNA-048

A Frog's Body

William Morrow and Company   New York 1980

JOANNA COLE
with photographs by Jerome Wexler

A Frog's Body

Morrow Junior Books   New York

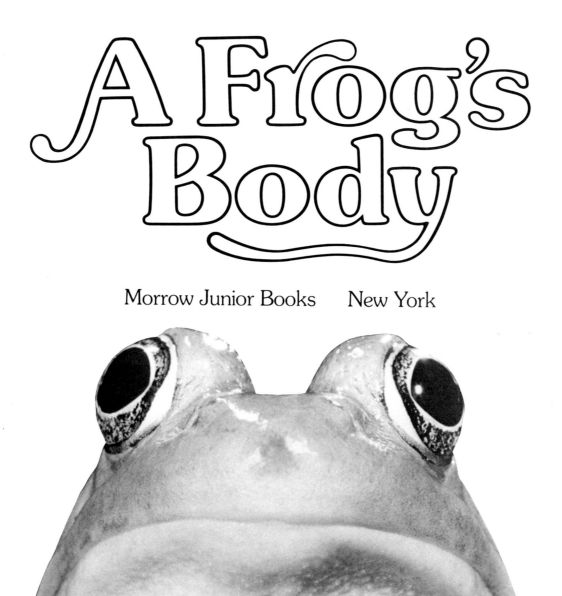

Design by Lucy Fehr
Diagrams by Terry M. Fehr

Library of Congress Cataloging in Publication Data

Cole, Joanna.
  A frog's body.
  Summary: Close-up photographs and text explain the details of a
frog's anatomy.
  1. Frogs—Anatomy—Juvenile literature.   [1. Frogs—Anatomy]
I. Wexler, Jerome.   II. Title. QL668.E2C78   597.8'7   80-10705
ISBN 0-688-22228-5   ISBN 0-688-32228-X lib. bdg.

The author wishes to thank Carol R. Townsend,
Scientific Assistant, Herpetology Department,
American Museum of Natural History,
for her very helpful reading of the manuscript.

To Philip

J.C.

To Keith Jay Lattig

J.W.

When you look at a bullfrog, you see an animal with a short, squat body, no tail, and moist, green skin. The bullfrog is an amphibian, which means that it is an animal with a two-part life. The early part of its life is spent as a tadpole, swimming in a pond and breathing through gills like a fish. When it becomes an adult, the bullfrog still lives in a pond, but its body is not like a fish's body. The frog can breathe air and hop around on land. Its body is suited to a life half in and half out of water.

The adult frog has many of the same inside organs as other land-dwelling animals. It has a heart for pumping blood, a stomach and intestines for digesting food, and lungs for breathing air. Because the frog's organs are so much like those of human beings, students study the frog to learn about the body.

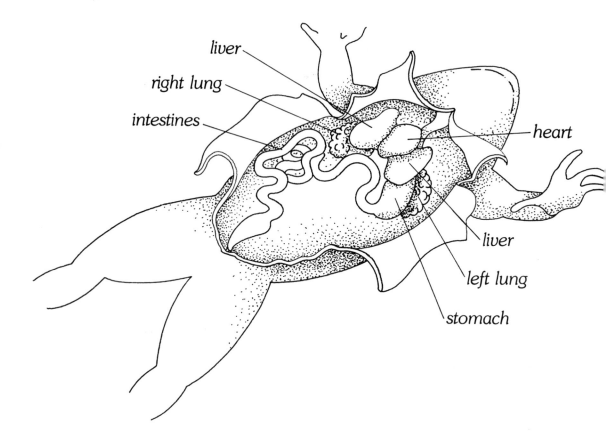

liver

right lung

intestines

heart

liver

left lung

stomach

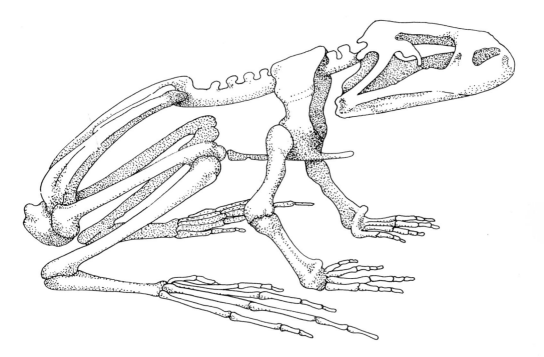

The frog's body is held up by a bony skeleton. A
frog has many of the same bones as other
vertebrates, or backboned animals, but it does not
have ribs. This lack of ribs is the reason that a frog
feels soft-bellied when you hold one.

Covering the frog's body
is a smooth, slippery skin
without scales, feathers, or fur.
This skin keeps out dirt and germs,
but it lets in water.
Therefore, the frog does not drink.
It gets all the water it needs
through its skin.

The frog also *loses* water
from its body through the skin.
A frog kept in dry air
for a short time
can lose almost half its weight.
When it is put back in water,
it quickly takes in the lost liquid
and becomes plump once again.

11

Like reptiles and fish, amphibians are what we call "cold-blooded" animals.

This does not mean that they are always cold. But they do not have any heat that is produced by their own body, as mammals and birds do.

Instead, they must get heat from outside the body— usually from basking in the sun or on warm rocks.

In an aquarium, a frog will bask in the warmth of a light bulb.

When the frog's body temperature rises too high, it moves away from the source of heat.

The bullfrog's coloring helps
to hide it from enemies.
Bullfrogs live in ponds,
which are mostly green.
The frog's skin is green too.

In a white aquarium,
you can see the frog easily.

14

But in a green pond, the same
frog is almost invisible.

A frog's back is dark in color, but its belly is light. This pattern is called "countershading." In the water, countershading makes the animal hard to see.

Seen from the top, the frog's dark back blends in with the dark pond bottom.

Seen from below, the light belly blends in with the light sky.

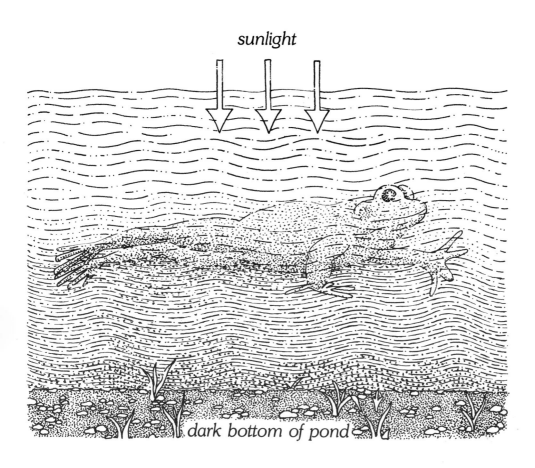

sunlight

dark bottom of pond

Seen from the side, the frog also blends in. Here is how the countershading works: The water in a pond is lighter near the top where the sun shines in. The sun lights up the frog's dark back, but its white belly stays in shadow. So the back seems lighter than it really is, and the belly seems darker. The whole frog appears to be the same shade, and it blends in with the pond water around it.

Most land animals get all the oxygen they need by breathing with the lungs. They expand the rib cage with the chest muscles and draw air into the lungs.

The bullfrog, however, has three ways of getting oxygen. The first way is called "lung breathing." Because the frog does not have ribs, it must push air into its lungs with its mouth. About once or twice a minute, it draws in a mouthful of air, then closes its nostrils, and forces the air into the lungs. As it does you can see the frog twitch.

In the picture opposite, the frog has drawn air into its mouth. The floor of the mouth is pushed out and the throat looks fat, because the mouth is full of air.

In the picture above, the floor of the mouth is pushed in. The frog has forced the air into the lungs, and the throat looks thinner.

In addition to breathing with its lungs, the frog also absorbs oxygen through the roof of its mouth. The roof of the mouth has a network of tiny blood vessels that take in oxygen. To get oxygen to this network, the frog constantly draws air in and out of its mouth only. This process is called "mouth breathing."

The third way a frog takes in oxygen is right through its skin, which can absorb oxygen from water and air. In the winter, when the frog hibernates on the pond bottom, it does not breathe at all, but gets the little oxygen it needs through its skin.

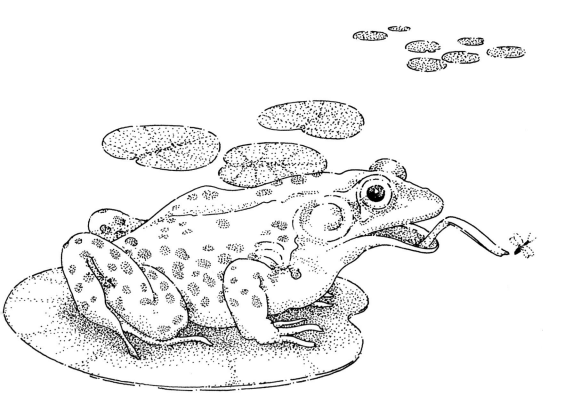

In addition to oxygen, frogs need food to live.
Bullfrogs eat insects, fish, other frogs—even small
birds. The bullfrog does not stalk its prey, but waits
quietly for it to come close. To capture flying insects,
the bullfrog uses its special tongue. When an insect
flies past, the tongue can flip out for an instant and
grab it.

Note: In this picture, the photographer is using a stick to hold out the frog's tongue, so you can see how it is attached.

This tongue is not much like a human tongue. It is long and sticky, and it is attached at the *front* of the mouth, not at the back.

When capturing insects or small animals
in the water,
the frog uses its mouth and teeth.
The tiny teeth are on the top jaw only.
They are not used for chewing,
but for holding onto live prey.

A bullfrog makes fast work
of eating a group of beetles
floating on the water.

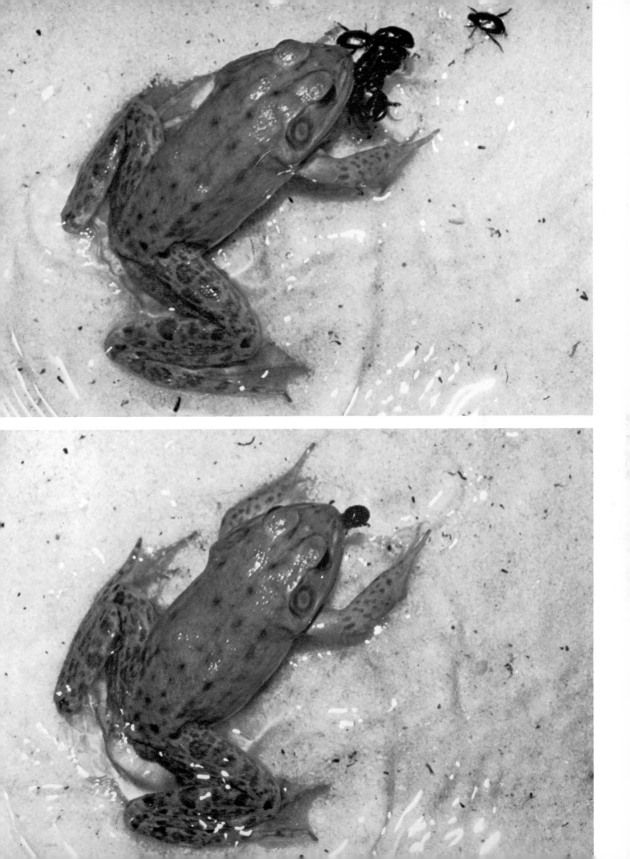

A bullfrog needs good vision to catch flying and swimming prey. Its eyes are large and can see colors and objects close up. As it does not chase its prey, it does not need to see objects far in the distance.

Bullfrogs cannot move their eyes very much, and they cannot turn their neck to see what's behind them. Nevertheless, they can see an insect coming from any direction, because their eyes are like a camera with a wide-angle lens. This kind of lens makes near objects look large and takes in a wide area. A frog can see in almost a complete circle.

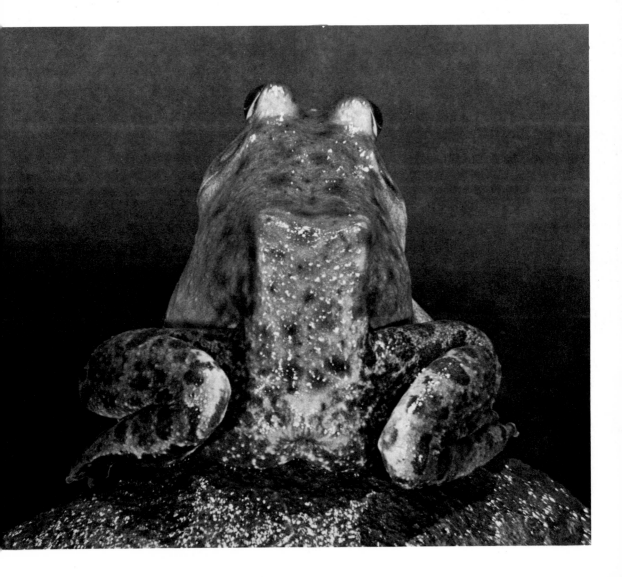

The bullfrog's upper eyelid cannot close. Instead, the frog has a lower lid that blinks and keeps the eye moist and clean. This special lid is a clear membrane. When a finger is placed near the eye, the lower lid will close. In this picture, you can see the lid half covering the eye.

A frog's eyes are not protected by a bony socket like those of most land animals. Instead, the eyes stick up above the level of the skull. As you can see, the frog's stick-up eyes allow it to see above water even when its body is completely underwater.

Most land animals have an outside ear. The eardrum, which picks up sound waves, is deep inside the ear. Frogs, however, do not have outside ears. The eardrum lies on the surface of the head. It is the large circle behind the frog's eye.

In the case of some kinds of frog, the way to tell the difference between males and females is by looking at the ear drum. The eardrum of the male frog is larger than the eye. Look at the pictures here. Can you tell which frogs are male and which are female?

The frog's ancestors were
prehistoric amphibians.
They were the first
animals with backbones to
live on land. They were
also the first animals
with four legs.
Scientists call four-legged
animals "tetrapods," which
means "four feet" in Greek.
Like their ancestors,
frogs are tetrapods too.
They have two front legs
and two back legs.
The short front legs
support the body
when the frog is at rest.

The bullfrog's front feet have four toes, which are used for grasping. There are no claws on the toes, but the ends are leathery and strong. A frog can hold on to a slippery rock or grab prey that is trying to escape.

The back legs and feet
are used for swimming
and jumping. Notice how
long and muscular the
back leg is. When it is
stretched out, it is longer
than the rest of the frog's body.

The back feet have five toes,
which are connected by
a thin web of skin.
The frog's foot is so well
suited to swimming underwater
that people have copied its design
for the flippers that
human divers wear.

These three pictures show the frog floating at rest,
swimming slowly, and swimming at top speed. Notice
how the frog's body becomes more and more
streamlined the faster it goes.

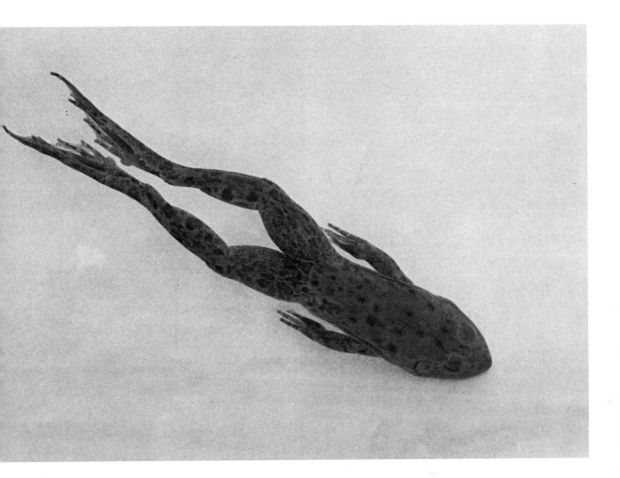

When a bullfrog swims fast, it folds its front legs
against its body to get them out of the way. Then it
frog kicks with its strong back legs. The webbed feet
push against the water and send the frog swiftly
ahead.

On land, the frog's usual method of getting around is by hopping and jumping. The bullfrog often jumps more than twenty times the length of its body.

Bullfrogs hardly ever walk,
but here are some rare pictures
of one taking a stroll.
You can see that it walks like
other four-legged animals.
That is, opposite front and
back legs go forward and back at
the same time. A four-legged
animal keeps its balance best
in this way.

Like all living things, frogs must bear young in order for the species to survive. To reproduce, the male and female frogs mate. Frogs have no sex organs outside the body. Both have a simple opening called a "cloaca." Eggs, sperm, and body wastes all pass through the cloaca.

MALE

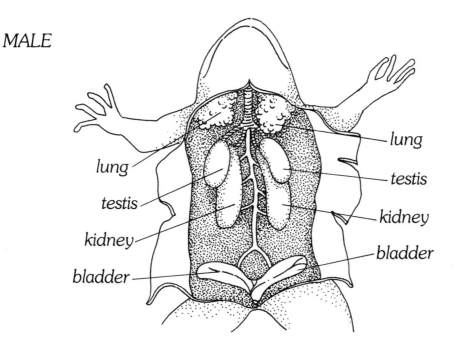

lung

testis

kidney

bladder

lung

testis

kidney

bladder

Inside the body, however, the male and female frogs are different. The male has two testes, the organs that produce sperm. The female has two ovaries, the organs that produce eggs.

FEMALE

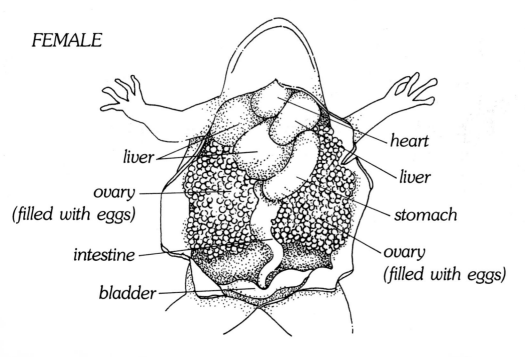

liver

ovary
(filled with eggs)

intestine

bladder

heart

liver

stomach

ovary
(filled with eggs)

During the spring mating season,
the male bullfrog makes a loud
bellowing croak to call the female.
He does so by forcing air
back and forth between the mouth
and the lungs.
The vocal cords in the throat make
the sound as the air passes over them.
Because the nostrils are kept closed,
the frog may be underwater
when it calls.
The frogs mate in water.
The male mounts the female
and grasps her body with his
forelegs.
As the female lays the eggs,
the male lets out sperm over them.
The fertilized eggs will hatch
into tadpoles.

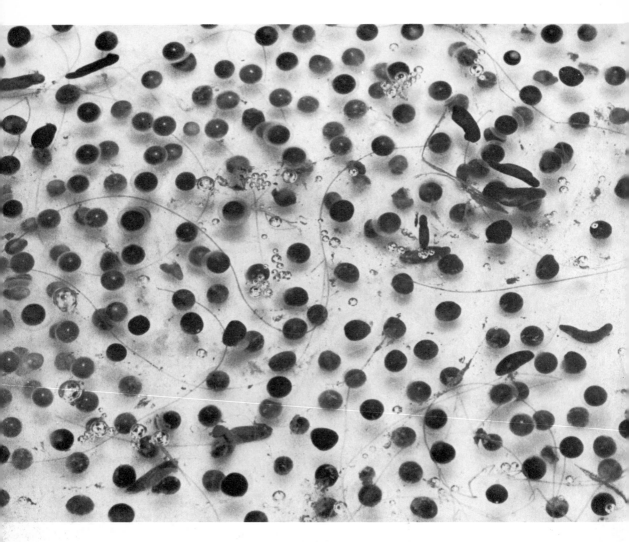

Here you can see some newly hatched tadpoles swimming among the eggs. A tadpole seems more like a fish than a frog. But as it grows, there is a great change in a tadpole. It grows legs, loses its tail, and develops lungs. Eventually it changes completely into an adult frog with the special body of an amphibian.

46

47

Born in Newark, New Jersey, Joanna Cole grew up in East Orange. After attending the University of Massachusetts and Indiana University, she earned a B.A. degree in psychology at the City College of New York. Later she took graduate courses in elementary education at New York University and served for one year in a Brooklyn elementary school as a librarian. Mrs. Cole now is a children's book editor and lives in New York City with her husband and daughter.

Jerome Wexler was born in New York City, where he attended Pratt Institute. Later he studied at the University of Connecticut. His interest in photography started when he was in the ninth grade. After service in World War II, he worked for the State Department in Europe as a photographer. Returning to the United States, he specialized in photographing farming techniques, and the pictures he made have been published throughout the world. Since then he has illustrated a number of children's books with his photographs of plants and animals.

At present, Mr. Wexler lives in Madison, Connecticut.